GUGLIELMO MARCONI

GUGLIELMO MARCONI

INVENTOR OF WIRELESS TECHNOLOGY

LIZ SONNEBORN

FRANKLIN WATTS
A Division of Scholastic Inc.
New York Toronto London Auckland Sydney
Mexico City New Delhi Hong Kong
Danbury, Connecticut

All Photographs © 2005 by Marconi Corporation plc except ©: Corbis Images: 21, 26, 58, 63, 87, 90 (Bettmann), 15, 84 (Hulton-Deutsch Collection), 81, 82 (Underwood & Underwood), 36 (Nik Wheeler); Getty Images/Time Life Pictures: 100; Library of Congress: cover, 2, 64, 78.

Library of Congress Cataloging-in-Publication Data
Sonneborn, Liz.
  Guglielmo Marconi : inventor of wireless technology / Liz Sonneborn.
     p. cm. — (Great life stories)
  Includes bibliographical references and index.
  ISBN 0-531-16752-6
  1. Marconi, Guglielmo, marchese, 1874–1937—Juvenile literature. 2. Inventors—Italy—Biography—Juvenile literature. 3. Wireless communication systems—History—Juvenile literature. I. Title. II. Series.
  TK5739.M3S66 2005
  621.384'092—dc22   2004030438

Printed in the United States of America.
1 2 3 4 5 6 7 8 9 10 R 14 13 12 11 10 09 08 07 06 05

CONTENTS

An early pioneer in wireless telegraphy, William H. Preece originated his own system in 1892. His most important contribution in this field was his

ONE

AN INVENTOR'S BOYHOOD

On December 12, 1896, a crowd gathered in London's Toynbee Hall. The audience had ventured out into the cold night's air to hear a lecture. The speaker was Sir William Preece, one of England's most notable scientists. The title of his lecture was "Telegraphy without Wires."

When Preece took the stage, the hall fell silent. Sixty-two years old with a long, bushy beard, Preece had a natural command over the audience. He explained that his talk would focus on new and exciting experiments performed by an Italian inventor, whom he then introduced to the crowd. Gesturing to a small, well-dressed Italian gentleman, Preece announced, "This young man is Signor Guglielmo Marconi, who is present here today and who will be able to repeat some of these experiments for you in miniature."

On the stage with Preece, Marconi set up a black metal box, which contained a telegraph key. Marconi then picked up a second box and carried it to the back of the room. Inside was an electrical device attached to a bell. The audience watched as Preece pressed down the key in the box on stage. At the same instant, the bell rang out from the other box, yards away.

The people in Toynbee Hall had never seen anything like this before. How, they wondered, could the key in Preece's box activate the bell in Marconi's when the two boxes had no wire running between them? Some, no doubt, thought it had to be a trick, something a magician might dream up.

In fact, the crowd had just witnessed the first public demonstration of wireless technology. Within a few years Marconi would become famous around the globe. And within a few decades, his invention would change the world of communication, paving the way for a host of other technological miracles, including radar, radio, and television.

This black metal box was used during the first demonstration of wireless technology. It is known as a coherer receiver.

VILLA GRIFFONE

Guglielmo Marconi came from a distinguished Italian family. The Marconis of Bologna were not extremely wealthy, but because of their extensive landholdings, they enjoyed a high status in the city and countryside surrounding it. As the son of a landowner, Marconi's father, Giuseppe, was expected to attend schools operated by the Catholic Church. For a time he went to a seminary to study to be a priest. While still a young man, however, Giuseppe decided to quit the seminary and abandon the priesthood.

Living in Bologna, Giuseppe Marconi met Giulia de Renoli, the daughter of a rich banker. The two married and had a son, Luigi, nine months later. Giulia died in childbirth, leaving Giuseppe a young widower with a child to raise. His father, Domenico, moved into his household to help out. Domenico, however, disliked city life, so Giuseppe agreed to move to the village of Pontecchio about 10 miles (16 kilometers) outside of Bologna.

The Marconis bought a large country house, or villa. Built in about 1600, Villa Griffone was a stately building, with three stories topped by an attic. Its balcony offered a view of lush lands dotted with fields, orchards, and vineyards tended by tenant farmers. The community around Villa Griffone was largely untouched by the modern world. The people living there farmed the land much as their ancestors had for centuries.

After his wife's death, Giuseppe remained close to his in-laws. While visiting them, he met a beautiful young woman named Annie Jameson. A friend of the Renolis, her rich father operated a prosperous whiskey distillery in Ireland. Annie, his youngest daughter, had a stirring singing voice. Although her parents would not allow her to have a stage career, they did agree to let her travel to Italy to study opera.

Giuseppe and Annie fell in love. Annie returned to Ireland and asked her parents for permission to marry him. They flatly refused. Giuseppe was seventeen years older than she and had a child by another woman, enough to make him a less than desirable catch. Even worse, he was Italian, and they were suspicious of foreigners.

Annie pretended to accept their decision. Yet, when she turned twenty-one, she rushed to France, where she had arranged to meet Giuseppe. They married and traveled back to Italy together. They settled into married life, spending winters in Bologna and summers at Villa Griffone. In 1866, Annie gave birth to a son, Alfonso. Eight years later she had her second child, Guglielmo. According to family legend a visitor once made a remark about the baby's large ears. Annie defended Guglielmo's appearance, insisting, "he will be able to hear the still, small voice of the air."

GROWING UP

Giuseppe Marconi was a stern father. He demanded that his boys respect and obey their elders. Annie Marconi was much more indulgent, especially with Guglielmo, who was always her favorite. He spent many childhood summers playing with his brothers in Villa Griffone's orchards and fishing for trout in a nearby stream. Like Annie, both her boys enjoyed music. Alfonso played the violin, while Guglielmo mastered the piano.

Annie liked to travel and often took her children with her. During

Guglielmo's early boyhood, they frequently visited Annie's sister Elizabeth, who lived for a time in an English community in Florence, Italy. Guglielmo played with Elizabeth's four girls. Instructed well by his mother, Guglielmo could speak English almost as well as his English cousins could.

Because of their travels, Guglielmo's formal education was spotty. He was taught largely at home by tutors. Early on Guglielmo displayed an eagerness to learn on his own. He was especially fascinated by machines and how they worked. Guglielmo liked to take household objects apart and put them back together, often rearranging the pieces so the objects worked better than before.

Guglielmo also loved combing through his father's library. He particularly liked reading Greek myths, but his favorite books were about science. Guglielmo especially enjoyed a biography of Benjamin Franklin. It

Marconi (left) is pictured at age six with his mother and brother Alfonso at Villa Griffone.

described his famous experiment with electricity, during which he flew a kite with a key tied to its string during a lightning storm.

Guglielmo also pored over a collection of lectures delivered by Michael Faraday. Born in England in 1791, Faraday was one of the most famous scientists of the nineteenth century. In 1819, the Danish physicist Hans Christian Ørsted had shown that electricity could produce magnetism. Faraday set out to prove the reverse—that magnetism could produce electricity. Faraday's work led to the invention of the electric motor.

As Guglielmo's fascination with electricity grew, he began reading everything he could on the subject. He scoured all the leading scientific journals to keep up with new developments in the field. He jotted down notes about everything he learned about the latest theories and experiments.

From his studies, Guglielmo discovered the work of another British scientist, James Clerk Maxwell. Ten years before Guglielmo was born, Maxwell proved mathematically that electricity and magnetism were two aspects of the same force. According to Maxwell, electromagnetic energy traveled in waves moving at the speed of light. Light itself was one type of electromagnetic wave; other types existed but were invisible to the human eye.

Supportive of his interest in science, Guglielmo's mother enrolled him in a technical institute in Florence for secondary school. Shy and withdrawn, Guglielmo had trouble making friends. His classmates often made fun of him, particularly for his speech, which betrayed a slight Irish accent. While school was difficult socially, Guglielmo found it exciting intellectually. Studying at the institute gave him a more solid grounding in theoretical physics—something he would need if he were to conduct his own experiments with electricity.

IMAGING THE WIRELESS

While at school he met Nello Marchetti, a retired telegraph operator who taught him Morse code. At the time, using a telegraph was the only way to send messages instantaneously over long distances. In a telegraph system, the sender of the message pressed a key on a telegraphic device. Each tap on the key sent an electrical impulse along a cable. At the receiving end, these impulses were recorded with marks on a strip of paper. Patterns of short and long impulses represented letters of the alphabet. This system of communication was called Morse code after the telegraph's inventor, Samuel Morse. Guglielmo was so fascinated with

MORSE CODE

In 1838, inventor Samuel F. B. Morse devised a code to send messages using his telegraph. The code employed two symbols—the dot (•) and the dash (—). A short burst of current sent through a telegraph cable created a dot. A long burst produced a dash. Each letter of the alphabet was represented by a unique combination of dots and dashes.

A	•—	H	••••	O	———	V	•••—
B	—•••	I	••	P	•——•	W	•——
C	—•—•	J	•———	Q	——•—	X	—••—
D	—••	K	—•—	R	•—•	Y	—•——
E	•	L	•—••	S	•••	Z	——••
F	••—•	M	——	T	—		
G	——•	N	—•	U	••—		

the telegraph that he built a telegraph transmitter on his own when he was only sixteen.

Despite his troubles at school, Guglielmo's achievements outside the classroom made him extremely confident. He later confessed that even as a young child he had an "irresistible feeling that one day I would be able to do something new and great." He also had little doubt that in time he would outshine his classmates: "They will realize one day—I used to say to myself—that I am not as dumb as they think."

While clearly intelligent, Guglielmo was not a good student. At age eighteen, he took a series of examinations to earn his diploma. He passed only one. Without a diploma, Guglielmo's future was uncertain. As the youngest Marconi son, he could not count on inheriting his father's estate, so he was expected to select a socially acceptable profession. His father wanted him to attend the Italian naval academy. The idea appealed to Guglielmo, because several of his friends had joined the navy. With no diploma, however, the academy would never take him as a student.

Begrudgingly, Guglielmo returned home, unsure of what to do next. He continued studying electricity, to his father's dismay. Giuseppe Marconi thought Guglielmo was wasting his time. In Giuseppe's eyes his son's passion for science was nothing but fun and games. Giuseppe wanted him to concentrate on finding a respectable job.

In the summer of 1894, Guglielmo vacationed in the Alps with his mother. He brought his science magazines along for entertainment. Several had articles about Henrich Hertz, a young German physicist who had died suddenly earlier in the year. An expert in electromagnetism, Hertz had studied Maxwell's equations. In theory, Maxwell was right about electromagnetic waves, but Hertz wanted to prove the validity of Maxwell's ideas through laboratory experiments. Hertz created a device, made of two metal balls with a gap between them, that was attached to a battery. The electrical charge from the battery produced a spark between the balls. Hertz showed that the spark transmitted an electromagnetic wave that traveled invisibly through the air. When it reached a receiver Hertz had built, the wave produced a spark.

Hertz's work also produced a spark in the brain of Guglielmo Marconi. Marconi later wrote that it inspired him with "an idea . . . so elementary, so simple in logic that it seemed difficult to believe no-one else had thought of putting it into practice." He realized that the waves Hertz sent from his transmitter to his receiver could be put to practical use. Suddenly, Marconi envisioned a new invention—a wireless telegraph, able to send Morse code without cables.

The Scottish physicist James Clerk Maxwell did revolutionary work in several fields of study.

Heinrich Hertz, a German physicist, applied Maxwell's theories to the production and reception of radio waves. The term "hertz"—the unit of frequency in a radio wave—is named in honor of him.

TWO

DEVELOPING THE
WIRELESS

To young Guglielmo Marconi, the concept of wireless telegraphy was brilliant in its simplicity, but there were some obvious problems with the idea. Hertz had been able to transmit electromagnetic waves to a receiver, but only over a very short distance. There were no guarantees a similar system would work over a long distance. In fact, most physicists of the time believed this was impossible. Electromagnetic waves traveled in a straight line, but the earth was curved. These physicists thought waves sent from a transmitter would fly off into space long before they could be picked up by a receiver placed any significant distance away.

Even if these physicists were wrong, Marconi faced another obstacle. If he, a teenager without even a secondary school diploma, could come up with the idea, surely older professional scientists could as well. He figured somewhere in the world other students of electromagnetism were working on inventing a wireless telegraph. And most likely they had far more education and much better equipment than he did. If Marconi was going to be the first to invent the wireless telegraph, he had to work fast.

A LABORATORY IN THE ATTIC

One of the articles about Hertz that inspired Marconi was written by Augusto Righi. A professor at the University of Bologna, Righi was an important authority on electromagnetic force. Given Marconi's interest in the subject, his parents used their influence to arrange a meeting

THE ELECTROMAGNETIC SPECTRUM

In Marconi's youth, scientists were just beginning to learn about the electromagnetic spectrum—an array, or group, of electromagnetic waves that exist in the universe. These include radio waves, microwaves, ultraviolet light, and X-rays. All electromagnetic waves travel at the same speed, about 186,000 miles (300,000 km) per second. They differ, however, in their wavelengths, which determine the amount of energy they carry. Electromagnetic waves with short wavelengths have more energy than those with long wavelengths. The radio waves Marconi experimented with had wavelengths billions of times longer than those of visible light.

between their son and the scholar. Lacking a diploma, Marconi could not attend the university. Righi, nevertheless, gave Marconi access to the school's physics library and laboratory. Although friendly, Righi was not encouraging about Marconi's work. He gently suggested to the young man that trying to send electromagnetic waves over long distances was a waste of his time.

Marconi was not easily discouraged. He decided he needed to test his idea through experimentation, and to conduct experiments properly, he needed a laboratory of his own. Marconi approached his parents, asking for space and money to buy equipment. His mother was happy to indulge his passion. His father was far more hesitant. He still thought Marconi's interest in science was at best a useless hobby and at worst a distraction that kept him from growing up. Even so, Guiseppe Marconi agreed to front his son the funds he needed to get to work.

Villa Griffone was the childhood home of Marconi.

The Marconis offered Guglielmo the use of the attic at Villa Griffone. Previously, the room had been used by his grandfather Domenico to raise silkworms. Moving the trays of silkworms to the side, Guglielmo set about assembling his own personal laboratory.

TRIAL AND ERROR

When Marconi began his experiments, he had some background in electromagnetic theory, both from his brief schooling and from his own research. There was no existing scientific theory, however, that suggested a long-range wireless transmitter would work. Marconi was working on a hunch. He suspected invisible electromagnetic waves would obey laws similar to light waves. And from the visible universe, it was clear that light could travel over a long distance. He valued this real-world evidence over the objections of theoretical physicists, who challenged his idea. As Marconi later wrote, "If we had attributed to the power of light only the possibilities offered by a candle, we would never have built lighthouses and reflectors."

At his home laboratory, Marconi first tried to replicate Hertz's experiments. He quickly repeated Hertz's success, sending an electromagnetic wave from a transmitter to a receiver several yards away. Marconi also set about creating his own coherer, also known as a Branly tube. In 1890, French physicist Edouard Branly discovered that loose metal filings in a glass tube would not conduct electricity (that is, an electric current could not flow freely through them). If the tube was hit with an electric charge, however, the filings would cling together, or cohere. Once the filings cohered, the current could pass through the tube. Marconi had a good reason to be interested in the coherer invented by Branly. It could serve as an on-off switch in his receiver, allowing the instrument to receive electromagnetic waves only when Marconi wanted it to.

Marconi worked hard to improve Branly's coherer. Through painstaking trial and error, he determined that the filings had to be very fine and approximately the same size. He even pinpointed the exact proportions of metals to use for maximum efficiency—95 percent nickel filings mixed with 5 percent silver filings. Marconi also handcrafted the glass tube that held the filings. He started with manufactured thermometer

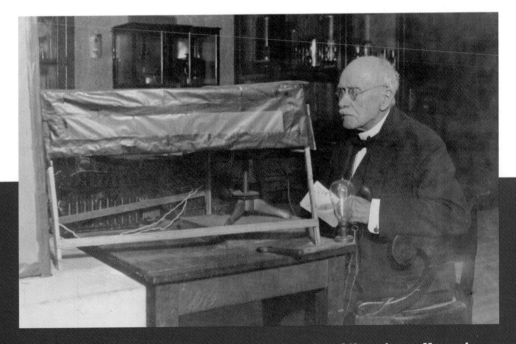

Edouard Branly, a French physicist, was the inventor of the coherer. Marconi worked hard to improve upon it.

tubes and heated them to remold the glass to exactly the thickness he needed. Between making the right filing mixture and molding the proper tube, he once estimated that it took one thousand hours to make one coherer.

Using one of his improved coherers, Marconi had a small victory. He rigged up a machine with a coherer on a circuit between a battery and an electric bell. At rest the filings in the coherer were scattered. As a result, they would not conduct electricity from the battery to the electric bell. Marconi found that during an electric storm, lightning produced electromagnetic waves that struck the coherer, causing the filings to cohere. Once they did, they allowed the electric current from the battery to travel to the bell. Hearing its ring filled Marconi with satisfaction. Through trial and error Marconi had proved that electromagnetic waves could travel to a receiver not just over yards but over miles.

MORE EXPERIMENTS

Alone in his laboratory Marconi worked at a fevered pace. He often conducted his experiments long into the night. His parents wondered

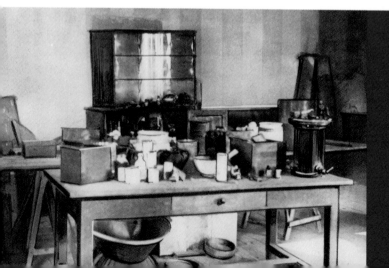

Marconi conducted many of his experiments in the attic of Villa Griffone.

what he was doing every day and every night, but Marconi remained tight-lipped about his work. He was especially hesitant to crow about his triumphs, fearing that he would set up expectations for success he was not yet sure he could meet.

There was one achievement, though, that Marconi could not stay silent about. Since his lightning experiment, he had been hard at work on a new challenge. He wanted to see if he could make the bell ring not with a natural electricity source but with a spark from a transmitter he built himself. Making a transmitter that could generate a powerful enough spark was difficult. But finally, late one night, the sound of the ringing bell filled the attic. Marconi was so excited, he woke up Annie. He made his bleary-eyed mother come to the laboratory so he could show her what his device could do.

In late 1894, Marconi's cousins came to visit. Afraid they would be a distraction, he locked himself in his laboratory, refusing to come downstairs even for family meals. His father was annoyed, but his always supportive mother left trays of his favorite dishes outside the attic door so he could have a good supper whenever he was ready to take a break. One day Marconi invited his favorite cousin, Daisy, for a private demonstration of his latest device. Daisy was amazed. She raved to the family about Marconi's miraculous invention. Hearing her story, even Giuseppe began to think his son might be onto something.

SENDING AN "S"

As the next year began, Marconi continued his tinkering. He worked on his transmitter to make it send out more powerful electromagnetic waves, while at the same time laboring to make his receiver more sensitive. Marconi also outfitted his transmitter with a telegraph key to see if his invention could be used to send messages in Morse code.

By the summer, his invention had outgrown the attic. Marconi kept the transmitter, now outfitted with an antenna, in his laboratory, but sent his brother Alfonso outside into the gardens around the villa with the receiver. Again and again the brothers tried out the device, hoping to improve its range. With the transmitter's antenna poking out the window, Marconi gave the key three quick strikes to send the Morse code for the letter "S." Marconi then looked outside. Alfonso, watching for three hits from a little hammer attached to the coherer, let him know if the receiver had responded by waving a handkerchief. Alfonso waved it vertically if the message had been received, horizontally if it had not.

From the attic where he conducted his experiments, Marconi could see his brother signaling to indicate reception.

On one clear morning as the summer was waning, Marconi decided to test his wireless telegraphy device over a far longer distance than he had ever before dared. Carrying the receiver, Alfonso and two tenant farmers walked across the fields of the Marconi estate, stopping about 1 mile (1.6 km) away on a hill, the Celestini, which was directly in line with the villa's attic window. Marconi could not see Alfonso's handkerchief at this distance, so the brothers agreed that, if the message was received, Alfonso would fire a gun into the air.

Once Alfonso and his helpers were out of sight, Marconi made three quick taps on his transmitter. He waited for a moment, hearing nothing. Finally, far in the distance, a single shot rang out. With relief and excitement, Marconi realized the experiment was a success. He was no longer an intelligent young man without a direction in life. He was now the inventor of the wireless telegraph. Marconi later maintained, "The calm of my life ended at that moment."

A HOMEMADE WIRELESS

Marconi's wireless system was composed of a transmitter that produced an electromagnetic wave and a receiver that responded to it. You can replicate this system using a 9-volt battery, a coin, and an AM radio. Tune the radio between two stations. Then hold the battery close to the radio and tap the contacts on the top of the battery with the coin. You will be able to hear a click on the radio each time you tap the battery. In this simple experiment the battery and coin transmit an electromagnetic wave, and the radio receives it.

This illustration shows how disorganized and disorderly the power lines were in

THREE

MARCONI'S BLACK BOXES

By the end of the nineteenth century, the telegraph had existed for more than fifty years, and the telephone was just coming into popular use. The two inventions had the same drawback—messages had to be sent through a cable or wire. Stringing these cables was expensive. In places where there were no cables, both inventions were useless. For instance, passengers on a ship in the middle of the ocean had no way to communicate with people on other ships or on the faraway coasts.

Marconi saw that his invention was more than a scientific marvel. It was the solution to a practical problem. The wireless, in fact, could

MESSAGES AT SEA

Before Marconi's wireless crews on ships were able to communicate with people on shore as long as land was visible. Blinking lights, for instance, were used to send messages in Morse code from shore to ship. Another popular naval communication system was semaphore. This system employed two colorful flags either held by a person with outstretched arms or mounted on moveable beams attached to a tower. Each letter of the alphabet was represented by a particular positioning of the two flags in the air.

revolutionize the communications industry. It would not only make sending messages at sea possible, but also make sending them on land far less expensive. Marconi also realized that developing the wireless for commercial use would take time and, more importantly, money. While he could invent the wireless alone in his attic, he would need help to market it to the world.

TO ENGLAND

Now fully behind his son's ambitions, Giuseppe Marconi began looking for support and funding for Guglielmo's invention. After consulting with several influential friends, he decided the Marconis should send a letter to Italy's Ministry of Posts and Telegraphs. Nervously, the family waited for a reply. Finally, a letter arrived in the mail. The ministry's response was a disappointment. In terse language it made it clear that the ministry saw little future in Marconi's wireless.

The family was upset and annoyed, but Annie Marconi proposed a new strategy. She suggested that Guglielmo look for help in England. Annie remained close to her family there, which had both money and influence in London. In addition, the city was then one of the greatest shipping centers in the world. The Marconis suspected that, unlike the Italians, the English were sure to understand how important the wireless could be to the shipping industry.

Annie wrote to her relatives, and in early 1896, she and Guglielmo boarded a train bound for the English capital. Among their luggage were two black metal boxes Guglielmo had built. Inside he stored a receiver and transmitter so he could demonstrate his invention to anyone who was interested. In London, Annie's nephew, Henry Jameson-Davis, met them at the train station. Henry had not seen Guglielmo since he was a toddler, but the two cousins immediately got along. Jameson-Davis was extremely excited by Marconi's invention. An engineer who had served in the English navy, he could appreciate the wireless both as a technological achievement and as a product that had the potential for earning Marconi a fortune.

RECEIVING A PATENT

After staying briefly with relatives, Annie and Guglielmo settled into a comfortable house in a fashionable neighborhood. With his mother, Guglielmo enjoyed the glamour of London high society. Because of Annie's family connections, they were invited to balls and dinner parties nearly every night.

Despite his busy social calendar, Marconi continued to work hard.

His first task was to repair the wireless he brought with him from Italy. An overenthusiastic customs officer in England rifled through his black boxes, almost destroying the delicate device in the process. With his cousin's assistance, Marconi found the materials to fix it. Soon the young inventor had the wireless back in working order.

Jameson-Davis also took Marconi to see one of the best lawyers in London. On his advice, Marconi started working on a patent application. If he could obtain a patent on the wireless, he would have a legal claim to his invention and any money it generated. For months Marconi worked on technical drawings and other supporting documents to convince the British Patent Office of his invention's worth. Finally, on June 2, 1896, he filed the final draft of his application. A little more than a year later, Marconi received his patent.

Just as important to Marconi's future, Jameson-Davis introduced him to A. A. Campbell-Swinton, a notable English specialist in electrical technology. Campbell-Swinton was impressed enough by Marconi to give him a letter of introduction to William Preece. Preece was not only

A.A. Campbell-Swinton was a pioneer in the development of television.

an important scientist, he was also the chief engineer of the English Post and Telegraph Service.

MEETING PREECE

On March 31, 1896, Marconi arrived at Preece's office, carrying his wireless device in two large bags. After exchanging greetings, Marconi showed the distinguished scientist his equipment and set up the two boxes for a private demonstration. As soon as Marconi's transmitter sent out a spark, the bell in the receiver rang out. An office assistant, P. R. Mullis, later recalled Preece's reaction: "I knew by the Chief's quiet manner and smile that something unusual had been effected."

Marconi, too, knew that Preece was impressed. The next day he wrote to his father about the meeting: "Yesterday I went to talk to [Preece] . . . who seemed to show extreme interest in my case and told me how he had tried to do what I have achieved using an arrangement different from mine without obtaining any good results. He promised me that, if I wanted to perform experiments, then he would allow me the use of any necessary building belonging to the telegraphic administration . . . of the United Kingdom." Preece also offered Marconi the assistance of post office employees as he continued to work on his invention. Among them was George Steven Kemp, a highly skilled technician who would become one of Marconi's most trusted assistants.

With Preece's help, Marconi arranged an open-air demonstration of the wireless for post office officials in July. He set the receiver and transmitter on two rooftops about 1 mile (1.6 km) apart. Marconi successfully transmitted a signal even with several tall buildings in the way, proving to his audience that physical obstacles would not block the flow of electro-magnetic waves.

Marconi's work soon attracted the attention of the British military. Representatives from the army and navy headed to the countryside near Salisbury Plain to watch another of the inventor's wireless demonstrations in September. This time, though, Marconi was able to send a signal over only about one-third of a mile (0.5 km).

Yet it was the Toynbee Hall demonstration held in late 1896 that garnered Marconi and his wireless the most attention from both the public and the press. Reporters hailed Marconi as the "inventor of wireless," much to the dismay of other scientists working on wireless technology. Some scientists complained that Marconi was not an innovator, noting correctly that he had borrowed freely from the work of others to build his wireless. Others said that Marconi's wireless would never be able to send messages over a long enough distance to be useful. The famous English physicist William Thomson Kelvin joked, "Wireless is all very well, but I would rather send a message by a boy on a pony."

Well aware of his detractors and competitors, Marconi was very careful when dealing with the press. He wanted to pique the public's interest in the wireless, but at the same time he did not want to give away too much about how it worked, for fear another inventor might steal his ideas.

INTERNATIONAL FAME

In March 1897, Marconi traveled to southwestern England for another demonstration. There, he impressed a crowd by sending a signal across the

Bristol Channel, a distance of 8.7 miles (14 km), a new record for Marconi. The experiment marked a milestone in wireless technology. It proved for the first time that waves could be sent over water, suggesting that the wireless could indeed be used for communication between ships.

At Preece's invitation, Adolph Slaby attended the demonstration. Slaby was a German scientist who had been studying wireless telegraphy. He was so impressed by Marconi's invention that he wanted his government to license the right to manufacture wireless equipment. No deal was ever reached, but Slaby remained determined to bring the wireless to his country.

Several Italians also witnessed the Bristol Channel demonstration. At their urging, the Italian government invited Marconi to bring his black boxes to Rome. First, Marconi demonstrated the wireless for a group of government officials, admirals, and generals. He wowed the crowd by sending a wireless message in Morse code. It read "viva l'Italia!"—long live Italy! News of Marconi's amazing invention spread throughout the country. Even the king and queen wanted to see it for themselves. They invited Marconi to the royal palace for a private demonstration. Marconi then traveled to the Italian naval base at La Spezia, where he sent a signal to a warship 11 miles (17.7 km) out at sea. This showed that the wireless could send a shore-to-ship message, even to a ship too far away to see.

For Marconi, his visit home was an extraordinary professional and personal triumph. Only sixteen months earlier he had left his beloved country, unable to find the slightest recognition for his work there. Now he had returned, not just as a famous inventor and an international celebrity but as the pride of Italy.

n London, Marconi's cousin Henry Jameson-Davis, an engineer, helped Marconi

FOUR

AHEAD OF THE COMPETITION

When Marconi returned to England, he was eager to get back to work. Because of the help of his cousin Henry Jameson-Davis, Marconi had plenty of money to pay for assistants and equipment. The money came from investors in the Wireless Telegraph and Signal Company, a corporation Marconi founded to develop and market his invention.

Most inventors have a hard time finding financial backing for their work, but Marconi was lucky that his family had so many wealthy friends in England. Acting as the company's managing director, Jameson-Davis had little trouble persuading many people to invest in Marconi's wireless.

In forming his company, Marconi gave up exclusive rights to his invention everywhere outside of Italy. In exchange, he received £15,000 (worth almost 12 million in today's U.S. dollars). He also received 60 percent of the 100,000 shares of company stock that were issued. The public sale of the other 40 percent raised the cash Marconi needed to transform the wireless from an intriguing electrical device into a marketable product.

The dazzling colors of the Alum Bay cliffs on the Isle of Wight have brought visitors for hundreds of years.

For Marconi, there were also downsides to establishing the company. The move angered William Preece, who wanted Marconi to continue to work under his supervision. It also put more pressure on Marconi than ever before. His investors were anxious to earn money from the wireless. The longer it took Marconi to develop his invention, the more impatient they were likely to become.

BUILDING STATIONS

In terms of earning a profit, Marconi decided that the wireless had its most promise in use as a communications tool on ships. On land, it would be hard to make the wireless more economical than the telegraph or telephone. But for ships far out at sea, away from connecting cables, the wireless was the only workable way of sending messages. Marconi had several problems to solve before he could sell a wireless service to navies and shipping companies. He had to increase the distance a wireless message could travel. He also had to make communication by the wireless reliable, quick, and inexpensive.

In November 1897, Marconi and his assistants moved to the Isle of Wight. In the summer, this island located off the southern coast of England was a favorite spot for wealthy vacationers, including the queen. Marconi rented rooms at the Royal Needles Hotel, a grand resort hotel high atop a white cliff overlooking the ocean. There he established the first fully equipped wireless telegraphy station in the world.

Outside the hotel Marconi's crew built a 120-foot (37 meter) antenna. Fellow guests at the Needles became used to hearing hissing and popping sounds as sparks shot from the antenna. Marconi, with the assistance of George Kemp, outfitted a ferry with a wireless receiver. They began experimenting to see how far out to sea they could receive signals from the transmitter based at the hotel. According to Kemp, Marconi disliked working in wet weather, but he had little choice. He had to develop a wireless system that would work between ships even in the middle of a storm.

Two months later, Marconi and his employees built a second station at Bournemouth on the English mainland. In 1898, several reporters were camped at Bournemouth to report on the final days of William Gladstone, a former prime minister of England. A blizzard swept through the area and knocked down its telegraph wires, making it seemingly impossible for the reporters to communicate with their newspaper offices in London. Marconi got the chance to demonstrate just how useful the wireless could be in bad weather.

Marconi helped the reporters send messages about Gladstone's deteriorating health and death to his station at the Needles, where the telegraph lines were still intact. His assistants then forwarded the messages via telegraph to London. The incident showed for the first time how useful the wireless could be in reporting breaking news.

Despite this success, Marconi decided to relocate the Bournemouth station, possibly because the management at his inn was annoyed by the loud noise of the transmitter. The new station was constructed nearby in the resort town of Poole. Marconi again set up business in a luxurious hotel. Although he often worked late into the night, he sometimes took time off in the evening to play piano in the hotel's common room, joined by his brother Alfonso on the violin and an engineer named Erskine Murray on the cello.

DRAMATIC DEMONSTRATIONS

By mid-1898, the British were hungry for news about Marconi's work. Reporters wrote glowing accounts of their visits to Bournemouth and Poole, where Marconi often took time out of his workday to demonstrate the wireless. Although inexperienced in business, Marconi could see how valuable this publicity was. It increased interest in the wireless in business and government circles, which also helped keep his investors happy.

In May, William Thomson Kelvin visited the Needles station. Once one of Marconi's greatest detractors, the famous scientist changed his mind about the young inventor after he saw for himself what the wireless could do. Newspapers reported that after Marconi sent a message for Kelvin, the scientist gave Marconi a shilling. He wanted to be Marconi's first paying customer "as an acknowledgement that your system is both practical and commercial."

Marconi received an even bigger publicity boost later that summer. At the request of the *Dublin Daily Express,* Marconi used the wireless to report on the Kingstown Regatta, a yacht race followed by sportsmen throughout England. During the race Marconi followed behind the yachts in a tugboat with a wireless transmitter on board. He sent hundreds of notes about the progress of the race to George Kemp, who manned a receiver on shore and telephoned Marconi's messages to Dublin.

Marconi's regatta reporting was popular with readers, including the British queen. Vacationing on the Isle of Wight, Queen Victoria asked Marconi to set up a station at her hotel and on the royal yacht, where her son Edward was recuperating from a knee injury. The queen and her friends loved playing with the wireless. In sixteen days, they transmitted more than one hundred messages. Another scientist might have resented his invention being used as a toy by the rich, but Marconi delighted in the attention. With obvious excitement, he wrote his father about the experience, adding that Edward had given him a tiepin, and Victoria had asked for a private meeting with him.

Because of these high-profile demonstrations, just about everyone in England knew Marconi as the inventor of the wireless. He was still no closer to turning a profit from his invention. By the end of the 1898, Marconi refocused his attention on his experiments. He set out for the English coast near the city of Dover, determined to send the first international wireless message to France. Marconi received permission from

TESTING THE WIRELESS

In 1899, two American reporters, Cleveland Moffett and Robert McClure, headed to Europe to watch Marconi at work. At the time, Marconi was trying to send a message from England to France across the English Channel. The reporters hoped to answer once and for all a question their readers were asking: Is the wireless just a trick? McClure joined Marconi in England, while Moffett joined his assistant George Kemp in France. Moffett dictated a message for Kemp to send to Marconi. Instantly, Marconi's wireless received a strange jumble of letters—rehte eht hguorht dnalgne ot ecnarf morf sgniteerg. Marconi was upset. He assumed from the gibberish that his equipment was not working correctly. McClure knew better. What came through the wireless was the exact message Moffett told him he would send—"Greetings from France to England through the ether," written backwards.

the French government to set up equipment across the English Channel at the French town of Wimereux. On March 27, 1899, Marconi tapped out a message from Dover, which Kemp received in Wimereux. It had traveled over water nearly 32 miles (52 km), a new record for Marconi's wireless.

Although consumed by his experiments, Marconi set them aside in October 1899 for an offer that seemed too good to pass up. The *New York Herald* asked him to report on the America's Cup, the world's most prestigious yachting competition. Marconi knew there was huge market for the wireless in the United States, so he was happy for the chance to publicize his invention there.

TO AMERICA

Taking his first trip across the Atlantic on an ocean liner, Marconi was met at the dock by a crowd of photographers and reporters. As in Europe,

In 1899, Marconi had the opportunity to go to the United States to report on the America's Cup. This gave him the opportunity to publicize his wireless invention.

readers in the United States were fascinated by new discoveries and inventions. With the nineteenth century coming to an end, people were thinking about the future and were enthusiastic about the technological innovations that would shape it.

While Marconi reported on the America's Cup, the American press reported on him. Newspapers featured descriptions of his experiments and illustrations of his equipment. They seemed even more interested in the inventor himself. Many reporters were surprised by Marconi's youth. One wrote, "He is a mere boy, with a boy's happy temperament and enthusiasm, and a man's nervous view of his life work. His manner is a little nervous and his eyes dreamy." Several writers remarked on how surprised they were by Marconi's neat appearance and modest demeanor. As Marconi later wrote, the reporters had expected to see "the popular type associated with an inventor in those days in America, that is to say a rather wild haired and eccentrically costumed person."

While in the United States, Marconi demonstrated the wireless to the U.S. Navy. During these trials the wireless failed to send intelligible

The *Transatlantic Times* was the first newspaper to be produced at sea.

messages, so the navy lost interest in Marconi's invention. Despite this disappointment, Marconi still believed the wireless had a future in the United States and established an American subsidiary of his company in November 1899.

Now a celebrity on both sides of the Atlantic, Marconi headed back to London on the *St. Paul,* then one of the most luxurious ocean liners. While socializing with the other first-class passengers, he met Josephine B. Holman, a young heiress from Indianapolis. The two fell in love and secretly became engaged. Both probably feared that their relatives would be against the match. Holman's parents would likely oppose her marriage to a foreigner without an assured income, while Marconi's relatives might have feared that his young fiancée would take Marconi's mind off his work, just as he was poised for a breakthrough. (As it turned out, they had nothing to worry about. Holman later broke off the engagement, mostly likely because Marconi was too busy to visit her.)

Even in the middle of his shipboard romance, Marconi found time to exploit another chance to publicize the wireless. A few days before he left the United States, the Boer War broke out in South Africa—a conflict that pitted British soldiers against settlers originally from Holland called Boeres or Afrikaners living there. Marconi set up his equipment on board so that as soon as the ship got close enough to the Needles station, he could send a message asking for war news. When Marconi got a response, he borrowed the ship's hand-operated printing press to create the *Transatlantic Times,* the first newspaper produced on a ship. The *Times* was mostly a stunt, designed primarily to impress his friends and fiancée. It showed, however, that Marconi was inching ever closer to ending the isolation of a ship at sea.

Sir John Ambrose Fleming, an English physicist, was Marconi's technical advisor.

FIVE

SENDING SIGNALS

When the twentieth century began, Marconi was back in England and hard at work. His firm—renamed Marconi's Wireless Telegraph Company in February 1900—was expanding rapidly. As Marconi's reputation grew, more potential customers became interested in the wireless.

To keep up with their inquiries, Marconi had to hire more assistants and engineers. The most important new employee was Sir John Ambrose Fleming, who joined Marconi's company as a technical adviser. Fleming was one of the most highly regarded physicists in England. He brought to the company an expertise in the latest theories about electricity, which Marconi lacked.

In 1900, Marconi was issued a patent numbered 7777. It became known as the Four Sevens patent.

While his business grew, so did the pressure on Marconi. The company was spending huge amounts of money, but not yet taking much in. By 1900, it was hovering close to bankruptcy.

THE BIG THING

Perhaps Marconi's biggest problem was a technical one. To use the wireless for communications, he had to send waves over longer distances, spreading the signal wider. As a result, if multiple messages were sent, waves could overlap and interfere with one another. In his laboratory at Poole, Marconi worked on the problem. Inspired by an experiment conducted by one of his detractors, Sir Oliver Lodge, Marconi developed a way of tuning the antennas in his transmitters and receivers to eliminate interference. On April 26, 1900, the British government issued Marconi a patent for his invention. Numbered 7777, it became known as the Four Sevens patent.

Two months later, Marconi made

an important decision. He became determined to tackle what he called the "big thing." In July, he met with his company's board of directors to explain his new goal. He told them he wanted to develop a wireless transmitter powerful enough to send a message all the way across the Atlantic. In Marconi's vision, transatlantic messages could be sent between the United States and Europe without a cable.

Trying to develop a transatlantic wireless was an enormous risk with no guarantees. It would cost the company a huge amount of money at a time when it was already close to financial collapse. Most physicists, in fact, believed that sending wireless messages across the Atlantic was impossible. They insisted that waves able to travel that distance would fly off into the air long before they reached the receiver.

Marconi, though, was sure they were wrong. He had already sent messages a distance of 80 miles (129 km), far enough to convince him that waves followed the curvature of the earth. He could not explain why waves behaved this way, but Marconi was always more interested in experimental data than in theoretical physics. He was sure that sending wireless messages over a long distance was possible.

Marconi made a persuasive case to his board of directors. They knew that if his hunch was right, the Marconi company could dominate the market for marine communication. If he was wrong, the company would be left in ruins. It was a huge gamble, but in a tremendous show of confidence in Marconi, the board agreed to back his plan.

All agreed not to say anything about the company's new strategy. Marconi did not want his competitors, especially those in the United States and in Germany, to know what he was doing, for fear they would try to beat him to it. He also did not want to alert the public. Always mindful of his reputation, Marconi did not want to promise anything he was not absolutely certain he could deliver.

POLDHU AND CAPE COD

With the support of his board, Marconi threw himself into developing the transatlantic wireless. He first traveled the southern coast of England to scope out a location for a new station. He chose a site at Poldhu. His engineers set about constructing the first transatlantic station designed by Ambrose Fleming. Nearby, they built a smaller station at Lizard Point.

EERIE AND ALARMING

Arthur Blok, who worked with Ambrose Fleming building the Poldhu station, later wrote about the deafening noise that rumbled through the surrounding countryside whenever the station emitted a spark: "The eerie and alarming appearance of that spark . . . is something not to be forgotten. . . . [T]he roar of the discharge could be heard for miles along the coast. The local ether storm produced by this smashing discharge was also noteworthy. Every metal gutter, drainpipe or other object about the sheds on the site resonated freely and there was a minor chorus of ticks and flashes in consonance with the discharge. . . . [W]hen one climbed up a short wooden ladder that leant against the hut there was a tingling sensation whenever one's hand passed over the nails which secured the rungs."

In January 1901, the Poldhu station was complete. It featured an enormous antenna system that rose nearly 200 feet (61 m) in to the air. The station produced a signal about one hundred times more powerful than any built before. Early experiments with the new stations were encouraging. Marconi succeeded in picking up a signal sent from Lizard Point at his old station on the Isle of Wight—a record distance of about two hundred miles (323 km).

Once the Poldhu station was in operation, Marconi set sail for the United States. He was accompanied by one of his best engineers, R. N. Vyvyan. Together, they traveled in a horse-drawn cart throughout Cape Cod in Massachusetts, looking for a place to build an American station. They chose a cliff high above the ocean near the town of South Wellfleet. For Marconi, though, the site had one great drawback. Used to elegant quarters, he was unimpressed by the local hotel. He was so disappointed with its restaurant that he imported his own food and wine during his stay.

Marconi soon returned to England, leaving Vyvyan in charge of constructing a station like the one in Poldhu in Cape Cod. Vyvyan and his crew worked quickly, but Vyvyan had reservations about Fleming's station design. He wrote to Marconi of his worries that the tall antenna would be too unstable. Vyvyan feared that even a strong breeze would knock it down.

Marconi ignored Vyvyan's warnings while he continued his experiments at Poldhu. In July, he succeeded in sending a signal 225 miles (363 km). Although encouraged, Marconi realized he had a long way to go. A signal sent between Poldhu and Cape Cod would have to travel ten times that distance.

THREE DOTS

In late 1901, Marconi's project was struck with twin disasters. A storm destroyed the Poldhu antenna. A few weeks later, wind blew down the Cape Cod antenna as well. Marconi acted quickly. He decided the Cape

After the antenna at the Marconi Station at Cape Cod was blown over by wind, Marconi decided to build a new station in Newfoundland, Canada.

Cod antenna would be too expensive to rebuild, so he chose to set up a new station in Newfoundland, Canada. In the meantime, Fleming redesigned his antenna to make it more sturdy. While a crew worked on constructing a new antenna system in Poldhu, Marconi and two assistants, George Kemp and Percy Paget, headed across the Atlantic to Canada.

When Marconi arrived on December 6, he met with the governor of Newfoundland, who offered the inventor his full support. In a few empty rooms in an old military hospital, Marconi and his men set up shop. As the site of their new station, they chose an area called Signal Hill. They used balloons and kites to carry an antenna some 400 feet (122 m) into the sky.

Marconi telegrammed his employees at Poldhu, where they had already set up a temporary station. He asked them to send the same Morse code message for three hours every day. From Poldhu, they used a telegraph device to make three swift taps repeatedly—the three Morse code "dots" that stood for the letter "S."

At Signal Hill, Marconi listened for the dots through an earpiece. Day after day, he heard nothing. Finally, at 12:30 P.M., on December 12, three brief clicks came through the device. Marconi was stunned. He handed the earpiece to Kemp, asking if he could hear it, too. Kemp agreed this was something more than Marconi's imagination. He heard the three dots as well.

They kept listening. At 1:10 and again at 2:00, they heard the Morse code signal. In total, the pattern of three clicks came through the earpiece some twenty-five times. Marconi later wrote of what ran through his mind: "I knew that the day on which I should be able to send full messages without wires or cables across the Atlantic was not far distant."

THE RADIOTELEGRAPHY INSTITUTE

While still struggling to build reliable wireless stations, Marconi realized there was another obstacle to his company's commercial success. It needed to hire hundreds of wireless operators. No school offered the training these operators would need. The Marconi company solved their problem by opening the Radiotelegraphy Institute, the first training school in the world for engineers and technicians specializing in wireless telegraphy. The young men trained at the institute had to pass rigorous exams in order to become Marconi operators.

TELLING THE WORLD

Now confident that his transatlantic wireless worked, Marconi decided to release the news. He first sent telegrams to King Edward VII in England and to his family in Bologna. Then, on December 16, 1901, he announced his achievement to the press.

Throughout the world, amazed reporters wrote glowing accounts of Marconi and his work. The front page of the *New York Times* declared his transatlantic wireless "the most wonderful scientific development in modern times." Marconi was flooded with telegrams of congratulation. He attended a great celebration in Newfoundland before heading to New York for a gala feast attended by Alexander Graham Bell, the famed inventor of the telephone, and other noted scientists.

Not everyone was so enthusiastic about Marconi's news. Some scientists said Marconi had been rash in making his announcement. They speculated that what Marconi had heard in his earpiece was just natural electrical discharges in the atmosphere. Knowing that a workable wireless could put them out of business, cable companies also said they were suspicious about Marconi's claim. One company even threatened legal action to make Marconi take down his Canadian station.

Marconi decided he needed to offer more proof to his detractors. He boarded a ship with a receiver and had an antenna fixed to its mast. The ship sailed from England into the Atlantic. With the ship's captain as his witness, Marconi received messages as far as 2,100 miles (3,379 km) from Poldhu. News of this demonstration quieted much of the criticism, but having to provide this additional proof still annoyed Marconi. Many papers gushed over this latest display of wireless technology, but Marconi only said, "This merely confirms what I have previously done."

The tower aerials at Poldhu would permanently replace the original circular aerial system.

Marconi inside the station in Newfoundland after receiving the first transatlantic wireless signal.

WIRELESS MANIA

At Signal Hill, Marconi had proven what he had long suspected—that sending wireless messages across the Atlantic was possible. Now he faced an even greater challenge. He had to find a way to make it practical. Unless Marconi could discover how to send lengthy messages quickly and accurately, the wireless would be little more than a curiosity, and his company would never turn a profit.

Luckily, the three dots sent across the Atlantic had boosted his reputation enough that he had more support than ever before. Canada was particularly impressed by Marconi's achievement. The country's prime minister met with Marconi and urged him to keep his operation in Canada. As an incentive it offered him a generous grant to pay for the new station he wanted to build. The great inventor Alexander Graham

Bell also offered his help. He invited Marconi to set up his station on free land on Cape Breton Island in the province of Nova Scotia.

After Marconi chose a location on the cliffs above Glace Bay, Vyvyan was put in charge of building the new station. He was determined to make it twice as powerful as the original Poldhu station, which was being upgraded along the same lines. By May 1902, the Marconi operation had established a three-way communication system connecting Glace Bay to Cape Cod to Poldhu.

AN INVITATION FROM A KING

Marconi's life was a blur, as he tried to secure new contracts, oversee his staff, and keep his board of directors happy. He still found time to work in the laboratory at Poole. There he concentrated on a technical problem that threatened the viability of the wireless. Marconi needed to find a replacement for the coherer—the part of the wireless receiver that detected electromagnetic waves. The coherer, made from a glass tube, was very delicate. Because it was so fragile, the coherer made the wireless too unreliable, especially on ships, where storms could easily break the glass just when wireless communication was needed most.

After months of working through the problem in his head, Marconi figured out a design for a magnetic detector. As described by Marconi, the device worked on the principle that "a core or rod of magnetic material becomes sensitive to [electromagnetic waves] when placed in a varying or moving magnetic field." Marconi's magnetic detector was simple and rugged. In fact, he fashioned the first one in fifteen minutes from materials he had in his lab, including a cigar box and florist wire. In May 1902,

Marconi submitted the first of two patent applications for the magnetic detector. The device—nicknamed "Maggie" by wireless operators—became a mainstay of wireless technology for the next twenty years.

The following month Marconi received an invitation from royalty. Victor Emmanuel III, the king of Italy, was visiting England for the coronation of the new British king, Edward VII. He asked Marconi to travel back to Italy with him aboard the *Carlo Alberto,* one of the best ships in the Italian navy. During the trip, Marconi could carry out experiments with the ship's six-hundred-man crew at his disposal.

Marconi was pleased with the king's offer. Despite his years spent in England, he was still a loyal Italian citizen. Recognition of his work from

The king of Italy asked Marconi to accompany him on the Italian navy's best ship, the *Carlo Alberto.*

Marconi and King Victor Emmanuel III traveled to Russia to see Czar Nicholas II. While there, Marconi gave the two men a demonstration of his wireless technology.

the Italian king was, in Marconi's eyes, an especially meaningful honor.

Before the *Carlo Alberto* headed for Italy, the king made a change in plans. Prince Edward fell ill, and his coronation was postponed. Victor Emmanuel decided to take his ship to Russia to visit the czar, Nicholas II, rather than wait in England for Edward's recovery. While en route, Marconi, assisted by Kemp, conducted a series of experiments.

When he reached Russia, Marconi took time off to enjoy the czar's hospitality, attending a number of lavish royal dinners. He also gave Victor Emmanuel and Nicholas a private demonstration of the wireless aboard the *Carlo Alberto*. After Marconi explained how his invention worked, a message came through the receiver that ended with "Long live the czar of Russia, long live the king of Italy." The monarchs were impressed, though Marconi had to confess the message did not come from Poldhu, which he had not been able to reach by wireless for days. It was actually sent from a transmitter attached to the prow of the ship.

IN ITALY

The *Carlo Alberto* continued on, stopping in England and then traveling to Italy. Marconi took a train to Rome, where he was met by screaming crowds. So many people flooded onto the tracks that his train had to stop a half mile from the platform.

While in Italy, Marconi continued his work. He wanted to see whether he could receive a message from Poldhu through the mountainous terrain that separated Italy and England. Setting up the *Carlo Alberto* in a direct line with the Poldhu station, Marconi began his experiment. In the early morning hours of September 4, the receiver clicked three times, recording the letter "S" in Morse code on its paper tape. The waves sent from Poldhu, traveling through the mountains in a dense fog, had reached Marconi's instrument.

Marconi was eager to stage another demonstration for Victor Emmanuel. He asked his staff at Poldhu to send a message of greeting to the Italian king. At first the message came through clearly, but soon all the tape was picking up was gibberish. Marconi determined that the problem was not with his equipment but with the inexperienced telegraph operator who was tapping out the text. In a rare fit of anger, he slammed his receiver on the table.

Despite this embarrassment, Marconi was energized by his stay in Italy. During an interview with a journalist, he was asked whether he could send a message around the world. With complete conviction, he declared that someday he could. Marconi explained, "It's simply a question of increasing the power of the transmitting station. The principle is absolute and knows no obstacles." The trip to Italy also gave him a chance to see his family in Bologna. Because of Giuseppe's ill health, the Marconis had moved from the villa to the city of Bologna to be closer to his doctors. The visit between Giuseppe and Guglielmo was their last. Giuseppe died a year and half later, in March 1904.

TWENTY-SEVEN WORDS ACROSS THE ATLANTIC

In late September 1902, Marconi headed back to England, then sailed across the Atlantic to Nova Scotia. By the time he arrived at Glace Bay, Vyvyan's work on the station was complete. The living quarters were rustic, and the weather was cold. Marconi was afraid the conditions were lowering the crew's morale and making them lazy. He enforced strict discipline, insisting everyone follow a work schedule and limiting meal times.

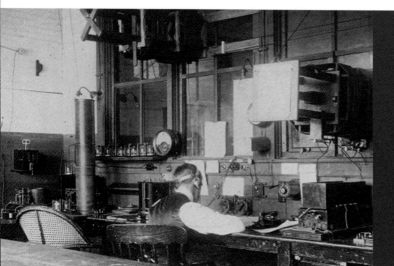

Marconi was strict with the workers at the Marconi wireless station at Glace Bay.

Marconi determined the Glace Bay station was ready to transmit transatlantic wireless messages. On November 19, he began sending signals to Poldhu, constantly readjusting his equipment. Nine days later the English station started receiving signals, but they were not readable. Marconi continued his adjustments. Two weeks later he was able to receive readable signals for two hours at a time.

Marconi then decided it was time to go public with his latest achievement. He invited George Parkin, a writer for the *London Times,* to witness the transmission of a twenty-seven-word message from Glace Bay to Poldhu. On December 15, Marconi sent the message at 1:00 in the morning. Marconi heard nothing back. He tried again at 6:00, but again there was no response. Marconi waited throughout the day for the sun to go down, because for reasons he did not understand, the sun's rays seemed to interfere with wireless transmissions.

At 10:00 P.M. that night, he resumed transmitting. This time Marconi immediately got a response from Poldhu. His men there had received every word. At Glace Bay, the engineers and technicians went wild at the news. They ran into the snow, jumping and cheering, even though it was −10 degrees Fahrenheit (−23 degrees Celsius)

Marconi brought everyone inside to the dining room. In front of a fire, he asked them all to stay quiet about what they had done. He wanted to send three more messages before the news leaked out. Marconi sent one to the king of Italy and one to the king of Britain, both signed by himself. The third, sent to the British king, was a greeting from a Canadian official. At first, the messages would not go through. But after days of fiddling with his equipment, Marconi finally transmitted his letters on December 20. Parkin's account of Marconi's success was published in the *Times* and reprinted widely. Several reports declared that "wireless mania" was sweeping the world.

A NEW TRIUMPH

To further capitalize on the publicity, Marconi headed to Cape Cod. At the station there on January 18, 1903, he sent a message from President Theodore Roosevelt to Edward VII. Congratulatory telegrams flooded in from all over the world. The two post offices nearest to the Cape Cod station had to hire additional staff to deal with the overload.

After his technological breakthrough, Marconi had to return to England to discuss his company's future with its board of directors. On the way, he stopped off in New Jersey to visit the home of Thomas Edison, then regarded as America's greatest inventor. Invited for lunch, Marconi spent a morning and afternoon discussing the latest advances in

WIRELESS AMATEURS

In 1905, the magazine *Scientific American* ran an advertisement for the Telimco Wireless Telegraph Outfit. The product was a kit with everything needed to build a simple transmitter and receiver. The ad sparked a craze among amateur wireless operators in the eastern United States. Mostly boys and young men, the amateurs built their own wireless systems, which they used to send Morse code messages to each other. Another tool of amateur wireless operators were crystal sets. These crude receivers allowed amateurs to listen to wireless signals, including those sent from Marconi's early stations.

technology. Edison was so engrossed by their discussion that Marconi had to remind him about lunch. With his housekeeper away, Edison scrounged up a meal of cheese on bread, washed down with water. Marconi remembered the visit fondly for the rest of his life.

On his way to England, Marconi had another noteworthy encounter. On the ship, he met a young American woman named Inez Milholland. For the second time in Marconi's life, a shipboard flirtation led to a serious romance. By the time the ship docked, they were engaged.

In March 1903, Marconi presided over the annual meeting of his company's board of directors. They already knew of Marconi's latest successes at Glace Bay, but he had more good news for them. He reported that the Italian government had just hired the company to build a large new station, and that the Canadian government had paid the substantial grant it promised. The company chairman, Colonel Sir Charles Euan-Smith, added another, perhaps even more welcome piece of information: For the first time, Marconi's company had begun to earn a profit.

Inez Milholland was an advocate for women's rights in the 1900s. Her last words were "Mr. President, how long must women wait for liberty?"

By the early 1900s, Marconi (pictured here in about 1903) knew that his wireless could be used by news reporters, military personnel, and ordinary citizens wishing to send messages over long distances.

SEVEN

WINNING THE NOBEL

The next few years were busy for Marconi. Now that he had created a workable transatlantic wireless system, he had to concentrate on marketing it to governments and companies around the globe. It quickly became clear just how many applications the wireless had in the modern world.

Almost immediately the wireless emerged as a particularly useful tool in news reporting, military maneuvers, and personal communications. In August 1903, while again crossing the Atlantic, Marconi published a daily newspaper with news from the United States and Europe. Thereafter, all big ships published similar papers. In 1904, war broke out between Russia and Japan. Both sides rushed to order Marconi wireless equipment to keep track of their army and navy operations. In January 1905, the British

MEETING WILHELM

In May 1903, at a royal dinner at the Italian king's palace, Marconi was introduced to Wilhelm II, the emperor of Germany. Almost immediately the meeting turned awkward. Wilhelm brought up a recent incident involving his brother, a German prince. While traveling to New York, the prince used German wireless equipment to send messages addressed to various friends to a Marconi station on the English coast. He assumed the station's operators would send them along. But when the Marconi operators determined there was no emergency onboard the prince's ship, they refused. The operators were merely following the rules established by the Marconi company, which agreed to relay messages only if they were transmitted by Marconi equipment. Wilhelm II confronted Marconi, claiming that he had insulted the prince. Politely but firmly, Marconi reminded him that "[i]t is my responsibility to decide my company's conduct."

Parliament passed an act allowing for "Marconigrams" —personal wireless telegrams that could be sent between ships and post offices throughout England, where they were then forwarded to the addressees through the country's traditional telegraph system.

MEETING BEA

Although Marconi's work kept him traveling, he often returned to his laboratory at Poole. He occasionally made time for boating, fishing, and visiting with friends. Among them were the Van Raaltes, a wealthy family with a castle on Brownsea Island, located a few miles from Marconi's lab.

During one visit with the Van Raaltes, Marconi met a beautiful young woman named Beatrice O'Brien. She was descended from distinguished Irish and Scottish families. One ancestor was Brian Boru, who long ago had been the king of Ireland. Marconi was immediately taken with Bea and told her he was breaking off his engagement with Inez Milholland. Still, Bea hardly saw him as a serious suitor. Only nineteen, she thought Marconi, at thirty, was far too old for her.

Marconi was as persistent in romance as he was in work. He followed Bea to London and proposed to her. She said she had to think about it. A week later, she invited Marconi to tea and formally refused his offer. Later, when the Van Raaltes invited Bea to their castle, she agreed to come only after they assured her that Marconi would not be there. They invited Marconi without telling her. At this meeting, Marconi was finally able to convince Bea to marry him, even though her family was unsure about having an Italian in-law.

On March 16, 1905, Marconi and Bea were married in a lavish ceremony in London. Many important English politicians and nobles attended the wedding, which was covered as an important news event in the world press. After the ceremony the couple set off for a weeklong honeymoon.

The good times did not last for long. Even on their honeymoon

Marconi and Beatrice O'Brien were married in 1905 at St. Georges in Hanover Square, London.

Bea and Guglielmo argued over his excessive jealousy. Their relationship soured further when he insisted that she accompany him to Glace Bay, where he wanted to conduct some new experiments. Accustomed to a glamorous social life, Bea hated the cold, isolated setting. The troubles between the two only got worse as Guglielmo became less and less interested in spending time with his wife. The relationship followed a pattern seen in Marconi's earlier romances: He tended to become infatuated with pretty women, only to lose interest in them once they began to return his affection.

FINANCIAL TROUBLES

While his marriage deteriorated, Marconi became preoccupied with another problem. His company was again struggling. To accommodate its

THE THERMIONIC VALVE

While working for Marconi in 1905, Sir John Ambrose Fleming created one of his most significant inventions—the thermionic valve. The device, also called the diode, consisted of a glass tube containing two electrodes in a vacuum. It was called a valve because, within the tube, electric current could be sent from one electrode to the other, but not in the opposite direction. The thermionic valve's practical use was to amplify electric voltage. Its development was a hallmark in modern electronics, because it made broadcasting sound possible. Until recently, vacuum tubes of a more complex design were found in all radios, televisions, and even some computers.

growth, Marconi constructed a new station at Clifden on the coast of Ireland. He also built a large factory in England to meet the demands for wireless equipment. These and other expenses left the company strapped for cash. Cuthbert Hall, the company's managing director, complained, "Half my time is taken up in very unsuccessful attempts to get money, and a great part of what is left in seeing how we can do without it."

At the same time, Marconi suffered several personal blows. In February 1906, Bea gave birth to a daughter, Lucia, but the baby died a few weeks later. Soon after, Marconi himself became very ill. A bout with malaria left him bedridden for months.

Early in 1908, Marconi took drastic action to save his company. He fired 150 employees, including Hall, and took over as managing director. He also closed his factory and asked many of the executives to start paying their own expenses. Even with this cost cutting, Marconi had to pour his personal fortune into the company to keep it afloat.

Marconi (seated, middle) posed for this picture with his staff at Clifden station. In 1908, he fired many of his employees to cut costs and help keep his company from going bankrupt.

Luckily for Marconi, the company's fortunes soon turned. In February 1908, it began its first regular transatlantic service between North America and Europe. Sending Marconigrams between Glace Bay and Clifden, the service transmitted ten thousand words in its first month alone. Not all customers were happy with the service, though. Many complained it was too slow. Marconi's company responded by upgrading the stations at Poldhu and Cape Cod so they could send and receive Marconigrams as well. The company predicted that the four stations would soon be able to process twenty words per minute, bringing in an annual revenue of more than $4 million in today's U.S. dollars. To Marconi, the most important Marconigram sent that year reached him in September while he was in the United States. It informed him that Bea had given birth to another daughter, whom Marconi named Degna.

WELCOME NEWS

Marconi's company was recovering from its financial crisis, but early in 1909, fate gave it an unexpected boost of good publicity. On the night of January 23, 1909, the *Republic,* an ocean liner, was traveling through a thick fog off the coast of Massachusetts. Seemingly out of nowhere, an Italian vessel appeared and accidentally rammed into the side of the *Republic.* The ocean liner was in bad shape. Worst of all, the cabin that contained its wireless equipment was crushed.

Fortunately for the *Republic's* passengers, the Marconi operator on board, Jack Binns, was uninjured. After struggling to repair his damaged equipment, he managed to send a message to the closest station on shore.

The station alerted other nearby ships to come to the rescue. The *Republic* sank, but not before 1,700 passengers were saved. Binns became an international hero and was presented with a watch by Marconi himself to thank him for his service. The incident proved Marconi's claim that the wireless could be a lifesaver for those involved in emergencies at sea.

The year 1909 ended with more good news for Marconi. In December, he heard an exciting rumor, which he wrote about to Bea: "Some of the papers have said that I have got the Nobel Prize of £8,000. It rather makes one's mouth water to think about it just now, but I suppose it's not true."

Soon Marconi learned the newspapers were right. He had won the coveted Nobel Prize in physics. Established by Albert Nobel, the inventor of dynamite, the Nobel prizes had been awarded for achievements in physics, chemistry, medicine, literature, and peace since 1901. (A Nobel Prize for economics was later added.) They were considered the highest award anyone could earn in these fields.

When the Nobel announcement was made, Marconi was a little disappointed to learn that he had to share the prize with Karl Ferdinand Braun, a German physicist who had worked on many of the same technical problems as Marconi. Even so, winning the Nobel was an enormous vindication for Marconi. The honor was an extraordinary tribute, especially considering that he did not even have a secondary school diploma. It also silenced once and for all many of his most vocal critics, who often complained that Marconi was nothing more than a businessman. As a Nobel prizewinner, Marconi finally had unimpeachable proof that the world regarded him as not only an important inventor but also an accomplished scientist.

Marconi and Godfrey Isaacs, managing director for Marconi's company, attend the court inquiry into the sinking of the *Titanic*.

EIGHT

To the Rescue

At beginning of 1910, the Marconi company was again thriving. It held six hundred patents on wireless equipment and had built more than five hundred wireless stations, making it possible to send a Marconigram nearly anywhere in the world. That January Marconi also found a new managing director for his company—Godfrey Isaacs, an old family friend with connections in the British government.

Hiring Isaacs was an enormous relief to Marconi. He disliked serving as managing director. Marconi much preferred spending his time developing new technology and promoting his wireless than running the company day to day. As soon as Isaac was in place, Marconi took the opportunity to head off to Buenos Aires in Brazil. With the help of his assistant H. J. Round, he set a new record for wireless transmission.

Marconi succeeded in receiving a signal sent from the Clifden station over a distance of 6,700 miles (10,806 km).

Basking in the glory of his latest achievement, Marconi received more good news on his way back to England. He learned that Beatrice had just had a son, Giuilio. Like Degna's, Giuilio's birth announcement arrived in a Marconigram, addressed simply to "Marconi—Atlantic."

THE CRIPPEN MURDER MYSTERY

A few months later the Marconi company got an unexpected publicity boost through a bizarre news story reported the world over by the wireless. The story began in London at the home of Hawley Harvey Crippen. Crippen called himself "doctor," although he was not a

Marconi was able to send and receive a signal from Buenos Aires, Brazil, to

physician. Instead, he was a peddler of home remedies, including one that supposedly cured deafness. His wife, known by the stage name Belle Elmore, was a little-known singer with plenty of friends in the city's theatrical circles.

One day in early 1910, Belle disappeared. Crippen told her friends she was sick and had traveled to California to recuperate. He later claimed Belle died there. When Belle's friends saw Crippen's secretary, Ethel le Neve, wearing Belle's jewelry, they became suspicious. In early July, Inspector Walter Dew paid a visit to Crippen. Crippen confessed to Dew that he had lied. He said Belle was not dead, but was living in Chicago with another man. Crippen explained he had been too embarrassed to reveal the truth, and Dew believed him.

The following day Crippen and le Neve were nowhere to be found. Now doubting Crippen's story, the police searched his house and made a grisly discovery—a headless and limbless torso hidden under the cellar floor. The police issued a warrant for Crippen's arrest and had his photograph and description published in London's newspapers.

A few weeks later the photograph caught the eye of Henry Kendall. He was the captain of the *Montrose,* a ship en route to Montreal, Canada. The man in the photo looked like one of Kendall's passengers. He called himself Mr. Robinson and was traveling with his son. Kendall began spying on Robinson and his boy. He noticed the son's clothes, clinging tightly in the ocean breeze, revealed unexpected curves. Kendall also saw Robinson and his son holding hands in a way that seemed a little too affectionate. Kendall asked the Marconi operator on board to send a message to Poldhu that he had found Dr. Crippen and his lover, Ethel le Neve.

As soon as the message reached the police, Inspector Dew set out to catch the next ship to Canada. At Liverpool he boarded the *Laurentic,* a newer and faster ship than the *Montrose.* As Dew raced to overtake the *Montrose,* the London press published news sent via the wireless by Kendall, who pretended to befriend Crippen. Picked up by newspapers around the world, the Crippen manhunt became an obsession for many readers, eager for any new detail. Characteristic of Kendall's minute-by-minute accounts was a published message reading, "Crippen is having breakfast. Suspects nothing."

The morning the *Montrose* docked in Canada, Dew came aboard, his face disguised by a pilot's hat. He approached Crippen, took off his hat, and shook the murderer's hand. Crippen reportedly said, "Thank God it's all over," and held out his wrists to be handcuffed. In their cabin the police found Ethel, who screamed in hysterics as they led her away. Crippen and le Neve were tried in England. Le Neve was acquitted, but Crippen was found guilty and hanged.

The Crippen affair had a huge impact on the wireless business. Each newspaper account of the manhunt amounted to an advertisement

THE MARCONIGRAPH

In October 1910, the Marconi company established its own press agency. Its goal was to publicize the company and inform the public about its products. The response was so great that the agency started its own magazine six months later. *The Marconigraph* was the first magazine in the world about wireless technology. Although under different ownership, it is still published today as *Electronics World.*

for Marconi's invention. Demand soared as commercial ships scrambled to install wireless equipment. Within a year only the smallest ships were left without an onboard Marconi communication system.

ISAACS AT WORK

This publicity boon helped solidify the reputation of the Marconi company. But just as important to its growth were the efforts of Godfrey Isaacs to eliminate as much competition in the wireless business as possible. Marconi's rival, Sir Oliver Lodge, had long been a thorn in the company's side. He held a patent that he could use to challenge Marconi's right to produce his transmitters. Isaac doubted he could beat Lodge in court, so he instead decided to buy him out. By the end of 1910, Lodge agreed to give up his wireless patent in exchange for a generous sum of money and a job as a Marconi consultant.

Another continual threat to the Marconi company was Telefunken, a German wireless firm. When the Marconi company was negotiating contracts with various governments, Telefunken often tried to spoil the deal, claiming Marconi did not have the right to sell its services in certain areas. Luckily for Isaacs, the Marconi company had a solid legal case, because Telefunken was producing equipment that violated Marconi's Four Sevens patent.

Issacs also actively sought out new contracts for the Marconi company. To lure new customers, he convinced the Marconi board to construct a new, bigger factory in January 1912. He wanted it built quickly so he could unveil it the following June. In that month, London was to host a world conference of experts in wireless technology. Issacs hoped to show off the factory and the Marconi company's fancy new head-quarters to the conference delegates.

As the factory was going up, another unexpected event again thrust the Marconi company into the limelight. This event would prove once and for all that wireless equipment aboard ships was no luxury. It was a necessity that could mean the difference between life and death.

THE *TITANIC* SAILS

In early 1912, the most luxurious ocean liner ever built was preparing to take its first trip across the Atlantic. The ship was huge and outfitted like a palace. It had electric lighting and heating when these were still rare even in the homes of the well-to-do. For publicity purposes, the company that operated the ship invited several celebrities to take its maiden voyage. Among them was Marconi, who booked space for himself, Bea, and their two children. At the last minute, though, they had to cancel. Marconi had urgent business in the United States, so he chose to take a

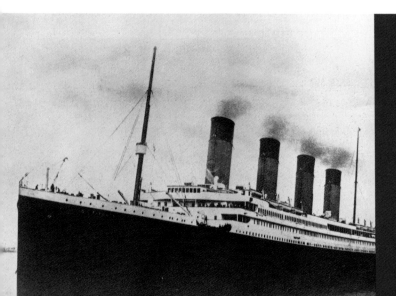

The British luxury liner *Titanic*, on its maiden voyage from Southampton to New York City, struck an iceberg about 95 miles south of the Grand Banks of Newfoundland just before midnight on April 14, 1912. The iceberg so damaged the *Titanic* that it sank in less than three hours.

faster ship, while at the same time Giulio became ill, and Bea decided to stay home. On April 10, 1912, the *Titanic* left England without them.

Like all large ocean liners, the *Titanic* was fully equipped for wireless communication. Unlike most, it had not one but two Marconi operators on board. The *Titanic* had many rich passengers who enjoyed the novelty of sending greetings to friends while on the high seas. The Marconi company made a good deal of money on these messages. To send the first ten words alone, it cost more than $16 in today's currency.

Jack Phillips and Harold Bride were the two operators aboard the *Titanic*. Both were trained by the Marconi company. Though only twenty-six, Phillips had already worked on several ocean liners and at the Clifden station. Bride, at twenty-two, had less experience, but he came recommended by Harold Cottam, an able Marconi operator and a friend of Phillips.

When they had few messages to send, Marconi operators on different ships often passed the time by chatting with one another in Morse code. If one became busy, he cut off the conversation by sending DDD. On the *Titanic*, though, Philips and Bride had no time for idle talk with their friends. Their workload was so heavy that they both spent eighteen hours a day tapping out passengers' messages.

DISASTER STRIKES

A little before midnight on April 14, Jack Phillips was still hard at work. An hour earlier, Cyrus Evans, the Marconi operator on the *Californian* located about 10 miles (16 km) away, sent a message to Phillips warning of large chunks of ice in the water. Phillips had relayed the information to the *Titanic's* captain. He also asked Evans to stop communicating with him because he was too busy to accept messages. Evans turned off his wireless and went to bed.

Bride, still in his pajamas, came into the wireless cabin and asked Phillips if he wanted him to take over his shift. They were soon interrupted by the captain, who told them his great ship had just collided with an iceberg. A few minutes later he asked them to send out the Marconi distress call—the letters CQD. In an instant, several ships picked up the message. The closest was the *Carpathia*. Its Marconi operator was Phillips's friend, Harold Cottam, who could barely believe the message, since the *Titanic* was thought to be unsinkable.

He sent back, "What's wrong? Should I tell my captain."

Phillips replied, "Yes. It's a CQD, old man. We have hit a berg and we are sinking."

As the *Carpathia* raced toward the sinking ship, Phillips and Bride frantically kept sending distress signals. The cabin began filling up with water. At 2:17, they sent their last message and raced to the ship's deck. Three minutes later the ship went down.

By the time the *Carpathia* arrived, about 1,500 *Titanic* passengers were dead. Among them was Jack Phillips. The ship's crew, however, was able to save 700 people. Harold Bride, found grabbing onto an overturned lifeboat, was one of the lucky ones.

After all the survivors were found, the *Carpathia* set out for New York City. Knowing the world was desperate for news about the *Titanic* disaster, Harold Cottam stayed at the wireless, sending to New York a list of the survivors. Working for twenty-four hours straight, Cottam was about to collapse when Bride took over. *Carpathia* crewmen had to carry Bride to the wireless cabin because his frostbitten legs were wrapped tightly in bandages.

Like the rest of the world, Marconi followed the *Titanic* story closely. He wrote to Beatrice, "Everyone seems so grateful to wireless—I can't go about New York without being mobbed and cheered—worse than Italy." Even so, when the *Carpathia* docked, he managed to pass unnoticed through the crowd gathered to meet the ship. Once the survivors were taken off, Marconi boarded the *Carpathia* and went to the wireless cabin. There, he thanked Bride and Cottam for their service. The two Marconi operators also received huge sums to tell their stories to the press. Bride's covered the entire front page of the *New York Times.* While heaping praise on the brave operators, an editorial in the newspaper declared Marconi as the event's greatest hero: "If Guglielmo Marconi were not one of the most modest of men, as well as of great men, we would have heard something, possibly much, from him as to the emotions he must have felt when he went down to the Cunard wharf, Thursday night, and saw coming off the *Carpathia,* hundred after hundred, the survivors of the *Titanic,* every one of whom owed life itself to his knowledge as a scientist and his genius as an inventor."

Because of the wireless telegraph, the *Titanic* was found quickly, and 700 people were saved.

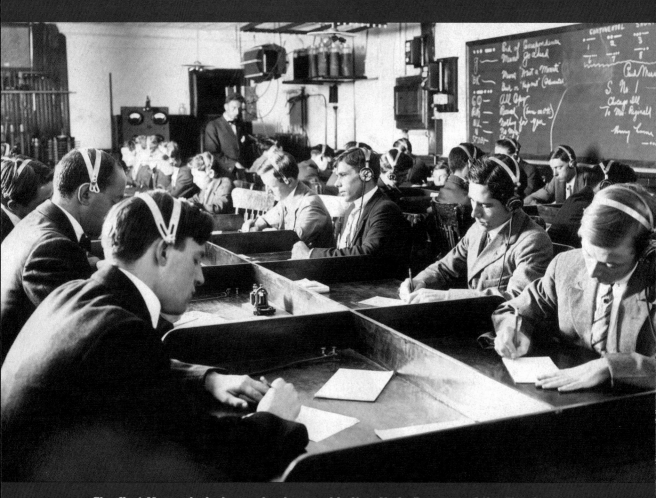

The first Marconi wireless school opened in New York. Because of the *Titanic* tragedy, many young men were eager to become wireless operators.

NINE

CHANGING TIMES

After the *Titanic* disaster, both the British and American governments held inquiries. They determined that the *Titanic* had had too few lifeboats, a fact that resulted in hundreds of needless deaths. The inquiries also pointed out the importance of the wireless to marine safety. These investigations concluded that ships should have someone manning the onboard wireless twenty-four hours a day. It was clear that if the sole operator of the *Californian,* the ship closest to the *Titanic,* had been awake and at work when the *Titanic* hit the iceberg, many more lives could have been saved.

The role the wireless played in the rescue had once again proved the worth of Marconi's invention. On the heels of this triumph, however, Marconi was to experience one of the most difficult periods of his life.

Lord Rufus Daniel Isaacs, the attorney general of England, was suspected of receiving inside information about Marconi stock from his brother Godfrey Isaacs.

About to enter his forties, Marconi would soon find himself plagued by personal struggles and scandal, while at the same time his world was plunged into a devastating war.

AN ACCIDENT AND A SCANDAL

In the summer of 1912, Marconi and his wife left England and headed off to Italy. Marconi chose to take the trip by automobile, then still a fairly novel form of transportation. Although he hired a chauffeur to drive his brand-new expensive Italian car, Marconi liked to take the wheel himself, often driving faster than he should on winding roads.

After checking on his Italian stations and visiting the king, Marconi left for the coastal city of Genoa, where he planned to take a ship to the United States. Marconi was at the wheel, Beatrice sat beside him, and his chauffeur and secretary were in the back seat. While whirling around a bend in the road, Marconi's car crashed headlong into a speeding automobile traveling in the opposite direction.

Miraculously, nearly everyone in both cars escaped with minor injuries. Marconi, though, was bleeding heavily from his right eye. The best doctors in Italy determined that the optic nerve was damaged and removed the injured eyeball. Always attentive to his appearance, Marconi was fitted with a glass eye so lifelike that few people noticed his infirmity.

While Marconi was recovering from his accident, his company was sent reeling by news reports accusing its managing director, Geoffrey Isaacs, of illegal dealings. The charges stemmed from the Imperial Wireless Scheme. A few years earlier the company had presented an idea to the British government. It proposed that Britain construct eighteen large stations in various countries that were then part of the British Empire. This network would allow ships in the British navy to communicate with each other throughout the world. The British government was hesitant to commit itself wholly to this expensive and ambitious project. In 1912, it drafted a preliminary contract for the first six stations. The contract was sent to Parliament for approval.

A scandal broke when reporters suggested that, while the deal was being negotiated, Isaacs told his brothers, Harry and Rufus, to buy stock in the company, which would surely rise in value if the contract went through. The charge was serious, because it was illegal to pass on such insider information. The allegations were especially explosive because Rufus Isaacs was Britain's attorney general. The accusation suggested a high level of corruption not only within the Marconi company, but also within the British government.

The British government launched an investigation, which dragged on into 1913. Although not personally charged with wrongdoing, Marconi appeared as a witness and quickly showed that he had not bought or sold shares during the negotiation of the Imperial Wireless Scheme. In the end, the Marconi company was cleared of all charges, but the scandal had tainted its reputation. The British government apologized to Marconi, and the king, perhaps as a conciliatory gesture, awarded him an honorary knighthood in 1914. But years later Marconi still remained bitter about the incident.

AT WAR

After the scandal, Isaacs continued to serve as the company's managing director. He had one of his greatest successes in that role in the summer of 1914. Under his direction, the company had sued the German firm Telefunken for infringing on Marconi's Four Sevens patent. Telefunken finally gave in and negotiated a settlement. Essentially, Telefunken became a minor partner of the Marconi company. The Marconi company could make deals around the world without interference from its long-time rival. In celebration, Marconi engineers were greeted as honored guests at Telefunken factories and research centers on July 29, 1914.

The Marconi-Telefunken war was over, but a far greater conflict was just beginning. A day before the Marconi employees toured Telefunken, Archduke Ferdinand of Austria was assassinated. The murder sparked World War I, which pitted Britain, France, and their allies against Germany, Austria, and their allies. Although Italy had an alliance with Germany and Austria, it initially remained neutral.

Marconi's life changed completely with the outbreak of World War I. Long considered a hero in England, he was suddenly treated with suspicion by friends and neighbors. Marconi had always been furiously loyal to Italy. Even though Italy had not taken sides, many British people believed it would inevitably fight alongside Germany. Not surprisingly, some feared Marconi would use his wireless technology to serve as a spy for his homeland.

The war was also a jolt to Marconi professionally. Under the Defence of the Realm Acts, the British government took over Marconi's company, knowing that the wireless was going to be an essential tool for the military during the

A painting showing the assassination of Archduke Ferdinand and his wife in Sarajevo. This event started World War I.

war. British forces also did everything they could to minimize Germany's wireless capability. After cutting Germany's undersea cables, they captured or destroyed eight German wireless stations in the war's first few months. At the city of Nauen, though, Germany still had an operating station that was then the most powerful in the world. From Nauen, Germany sent propaganda to countries throughout the world, including the United States.

To monitor these messages, the British needed thousands of new wireless operators. The Marconi company held classes day and night to train new recruits. The Marconi operators were able to intercept eighty million words beamed from Nauen throughout the war. For their efforts, some paid the ultimate price. Nearly 350 Marconi operators were killed during the war.

LIEUTENANT MARCONI

Marconi had his own brush with danger in April 1915, when he set sail aboard the *Lusitania* for the United States. The ship made the trip safely, although German submarines were traveling nearby in search of British ships. Fortunately for Marconi he did not take the *Lusitania* on his return trip, during which it was torpedoed off the coast of Ireland. Instead, he sailed back on the *St. Paul.* News that he was aboard this ship was sent to Nauen, fueling rumors that the Germans were plotting to capture Marconi. If a plot existed, however, it was never acted on.

While Marconi was away, Italy had joined the war on the side of the British and their allies. He rushed to Italy to help his country however he could. By the summer, Marconi had joined the army as a lieutenant and was placed in charge of its wireless service. While also working with the Italian navy, Marconi focused on developing new technology that would help the Italian military. One of his greatest challenges was creating a communication system for airplanes. Many early airplanes had room for only one person, so the pilot did not have his hands free to operate a telegraph key. Marconi, therefore, developed a wireless telephone system that allowed pilots to speak to ground stations at a range of 20 miles (32 km). By the end of the war, Italy had one thousand ground stations and six hundred airplanes fitted with Marconi's new device.

Marconi also served his country as a diplomat. After the United States entered the war in April 1917, he made goodwill visits to England

Pictured is a Marconi trench set from World War I. Thousands of operators were needed during the war.

and the United States on behalf of the Italian government. The next year, the war ended with victory for Britain, Italy, and their allies. Italy then asked Marconi to travel to the peace conference held in France, where he met with U.S. president Woodrow Wilson.

THE RISE OF RADIO

The postwar years were hard for Marconi. His plans for his company and his research had been placed on hold for four long years, and now he had to struggle to get both back on track. Separated for long periods from his family, his already tense relationship with his wife deteriorated even further. (There was one bright spot in his personal life, however—the birth of his daughter Gioia in April 1916.)

In other central ways that perhaps Marconi himself could not fully

Dr. Lee De Forest changed the world with his electronics. His two major inventions were an improved vacuum tube, which enabled live radio broadcasts, and equipment for recording sound with motion pictures.

see, the war had also forever changed the course of his life's work. One change was in his company's relationship with the U.S. and British governments. In the past, Marconi largely had the upper hand in their negotiations. After taking over the wireless industry during the war, however, both governments were reluctant to give quite so much control back to Marconi.

Even more important to Marconi's future was the rapid development of radio. Marconi had long been on the cutting edge of wireless technology, but radio broadcasting was never one of his real passions. During the war and postwar years, inventors and scientists in the United States came to recognize radio's promise. Drawing on the work of Marconi employee Ambrose Fleming, they focused on making regular radio broadcasting a reality. Because of their research, the click of Morse code over the wireless was soon replaced by the sound of the human voice.

FATHERS OF RADIO

Marconi is sometimes called the "Father of Radio" because his work and that of his colleagues led to some important discoveries that made radio possible. Several other scientists also deserve credit for their pioneering work in radio technology. Among them is American inventor Lee De Forest. He invented the thermionic triode vacuum tube, a device central to receiving radio signals that improved on an invention of Marconi's adviser, Ambrose Fleming. Another American, Reginald Fessenden, developed a technique to transmit audio signals. On Christmas Eve in 1906, he transmitted the first program of speech and music ever in the United States.

Marconi bought and renovated the *Elettra*. He spent many of his final days aboard the yacht.

TEN

FINAL DAYS

After the turmoil of the war, Marconi was ready for some peace and quiet. He found it aboard a grand yacht he christened the *Elettra* (meaning "electricity"). The yacht had been built in 1904 for Archduchess Maria Theresa of Austria but was seized during the war by the British navy. Marconi bought the ship and restored it from top to bottom, creating an elegant retreat. It even featured a state-of-the-art laboratory, constructed under the supervision of his loyal friend and assistant George Kemp.

For Marconi, sailing on the *Elettra* was an ideal getaway. He could go wherever he wanted, whenever he wanted, waited on by a staff of thirty. The *Elettra* also provided a perfect escape from the most troubling element of his life—his marriage to Bea.

In the spring of 1920, the disagreements between Marconi and his wife grew more serious. Marconi was having an affair, which he barely tried to hide. Bea was angry but agreed to go on a cruise aboard the *Elettra,* presumably their one last chance to save their marriage. When Bea boarded the yacht, she discovered that Marconi had also invited his mistress. Bea gave up on the marriage, and three years later, after she had fallen in love with another man, she asked Marconi for a divorce. He agreed with no resistance.

Marconi uses a wireless to perform direction-finding experiments in the cabin of the *Elettra*.

THE FLOATING LAB

Freed from his difficult family situation, Marconi spent much of his time aboard the *Elettra,* visiting with friends and working in his shipboard laboratory. In the 1920s, his experiments yielded some interesting results. One discovery that particularly intrigued him was that electromagnetic waves sent through water could be reflected back by a metal object. He believed it might be possible to build a marine radio that could detect the presence of other ships. On June 20, 1922, he gave a report to a group of American engineers in New York on his findings. In this lecture, Marconi foresaw the invention of "radio detection and ranging," or radar. Two decades later, radar would be an essential tool of the U.S. and British navies when they were fighting World War II.

Drawing on research he had conducted during the war, Marconi also became interested in shortwave wireless transmissions. Throughout his career, he had held that only long waves had the power to travel over long distances. A series of experiments conducted in the early 1920s changed his mind. At Poldhu, he constructed a shortwave transmitter with a reflector behind the antenna that concentrated its signal into a beam. He became convinced that, using the beam system, short waves could travel long distances as well.

Marconi also determined that, from a practical standpoint, shortwave communication was superior to long wave communication. Short waves required less power to generate, so they were a far cheaper alternative. They also could be more reliably transmitted and received during daylight hours.

Marconi convinced Britain to build several shortwave radio stations in different parts of its empire. In May 1924, he created a radio link between Poldhu and Sydney, establishing the first regular voice transmission between England and Australia. Three years later he finally completed the Imperial Wireless Scheme that had been abandoned years before following the Imperial Wireless Scandal.

THE COMPANY FLOUNDERS

Shortwave transmission was a technical triumph, but it also created some problems for his business. The Marconi company's stations were all built to use the long wave system. Converting them all to using short waves would be enormously expensive and risky.

Adding to the company's troubles was the 1925 resignation of Geoffrey Isaacs because of illness. Under Isaacs, the Marconi company had flourished, but it was also saddled with huge debts. After Isaacs's departure, a new board of directors was assembled. Most members were financiers instead of scientists. In the past, the board had largely trusted Marconi and let him have his way. The new board, though, did not want him meddling in its affairs. As a result Marconi became less and less active in company operations.

In March 1928, under pressure from the British government, the board agreed to merge Marconi's wireless business with the dying cable industry, creating a firm called Cable & Wireless. If Marconi had been at the meeting, he would have surely objected to the terms, which were not advantageous to the wireless end of the business. Nevertheless, the merger left Marconi financially secure, freeing him to spend his time as he chose.

MARRYING MARIA

After his divorce, Marconi socialized with many beauties. He was even briefly engaged to a seventeen-year-old English girl. In 1925, he met a particularly dazzling woman during a party on the *Elettra*. The daughter of Italian nobility and a staunch Catholic, Maria Cristina Bezzi-Scali was young and beautiful. He fell in love with her immediately, and soon Maria was a frequent guest on his yacht. After annulling his marriage to Bea, Marconi embraced the Catholic faith in order to marry Maria. Their wedding on June 15, 1927, was an international news event.

Following his second marriage, Marconi was less interested in his experiments, preferring instead to travel with his new wife and their friends. His research was also stifled by ill health. While on a trip with Maria in late 1927, Marconi had his first bout of angina pectoris, a painful and serious heart condition that had killed his mother in 1920.

This Marconi station at Bridgwater, England, was the shortwave receiving center for Canada and South Africa.

Although less active in the scientific community, Marconi was still considered a great Italian hero. One of his most loyal fans was Benito Mussolini, who rose to power in Italy in 1922 during the confusion of the postwar years. Leader of the brutal Fascist Party, Mussolini eventually consolidated his power, ruling Italy as a dictator. During the 1920s, Marconi joined the Fascist party. Mussolini rewarded Marconi by appointing him president of the Royal Italian Academy in 1930.

TRAVELING THE WORLD

In 1930, Marconi and Maria celebrated the birth of a daughter. Marconi named her Elettra after his yacht, a tribute to the place he and his wife first met. Since his divorce, Marconi's visits with the children from his first marriage had become fewer and far between. After Elettra's birth, Marconi largely ignored their very existence.

Despite his precarious health, Marconi, with Maria at his side, set off for a world cruise in 1933. They met with the president of China, visited the emperor's palace in Japan, and dined at the White House with President Franklin D. Roosevelt. They also traveled to Chicago, Illinois, to attend the World's Fair on Marconi Day. During the festivities, Marconi sent three Morse code dots from a wireless transmitter. In sequence, they were received at stations in New York, London, Rome, Bombay, Manila, Honolulu, and San Francisco. The signal then came back to Chicago, where it reached an automated detonator that set off a fireworks display. The signal's round-the-world journey took just three minutes and twenty-six seconds.

The following year Marconi took time off from his busy social schedule to conduct a new series of experiments. He was interested in using radio to allow ships and airplanes to navigate "blindly" when weather turned so bad it was impossible to see the path ahead. Marconi proved the viability of blind marine navigation. Covering the portholes of the *Elettra* with dark black curtains, he drove the yacht between two buoys positioned 50 meters (55 yards) apart using only radio waves to navigate any obstacles in his way.

Just a few months later, Marconi's health took a turn for the worse. In late 1934 and early 1935, he suffered a devastating series of angina pectoris attacks. His doctors cautioned him to relax, but Marconi insisted on traveling. In October 1935, Mussolini sent Italian troops into the African nation of Ethiopia, an act of aggression condemned by many other countries. Marconi set off on an international tour to make speeches in Mussolini's defense. He went to England, intending to read a pro-Fascist message over British radio. Accustomed to being treated with reverence in England, Marconi was stunned when the British government refused to give him radio time.

THE FABLED DEATH RAY

In the late 1930s, a rumor spread around Europe that Marconi had developed a powerful new weapon—the death ray. The device supposedly could kill people and animals and render automobiles, airplanes, and ships immobile. There was no truth at all in the rumor, but Mussolini was eager to keep it alive. Hoping to scare his enemies, he instructed his secret police to spread the death-ray myth to foreign spies.

Marconi (right, in uniform) made many speeches in support of Italian dictator Benito Mussolini (standing next to Marconi).

DEATH IN ROME

At the end of 1936, Marconi fell unconscious during a train trip to Rome. His recovery from this attack of angina pectoris was slow. He finally realized that his traveling days were largely over.

Although he was physically frail, Marconi continued his research into shortwave technology. On the morning of July 19, 1937, he went to his company's offices in Rome, where he met with his friend Luigi Solari. While the two discussed the experiments Marconi was planning, he started to feel ill and laid down on the couch. Mournfully, he told Solari, "There is still a lot to do in this field. I would like to have the energy I once had . . . the energy that I no longer have." Marconi had an appointment with Mussolini later in the day, but he became so ill that he had to retire to bed. His condition seemed to improve, but in the early hours of July 20, his heart gave out. At sixty-three years old, Guglielmo Marconi was dead.

News of Marconi's death soon reached every corner of the globe, sent by the radio technology he helped pioneer. Mussolini ordered a state funeral to be held the next day. Long into the evening thousands of mourners filed past his coffin. Tributes to Marconi were published in

THE PASSING OF MARCHESE MARCONI

MARCHESE MARCONI'S FUNERAL in his native town of Bologna. The scene after the funeral train had arrived

Thousands of people attended the funeral of Marconi. He was buried in a mausoleum papers all over the world. The *New York Times* devoted a full page to recounting his achievements. The story's headline—"World-Wide Tribute Is Paid to Marconi as the Benefactor of Many Millions"—stretched across eight columns.

Forty-one years had passed since Marconi first demonstrated his black box to the public. The very idea of wireless communication seemed magical then, but the world quickly caught up with Marconi's vision. Even after his death Marconi's work has continued to inspire new electronic inventions that have transformed the way we live. Radios, televisions, and wireless phones are just a few of the now-commonplace devices that Marconi helped make possible. Several of Marconi's obituaries compared him to Christopher Columbus. In a sense, he did discover a new world—the modern world, where there is no longer any mystery behind sending words through the air.

TIMELINE

GUGLIELMO MARCONI'S LIFE   WORLD EVENTS

1874 Guglielmo Marconi is born at the Marconi family estate outside of Bologna, Italy, on April 25.

1876 Alexander Graham Bell invents the telephone.

1879 Thomas Alva Edison invents the lightbulb.

1885 The first anti-rabies vaccine is administered by Louis Pasteur to a nine-year-old schoolboy.

1888 The Kodak camera is invented by George Eastman.

1895 Wilhelm Conrad Roentgen discovers the X ray.

1895 Marconi's early wireless system sends and receives a signal over a distance of about 1 mile (1.6 km) in September.

1896 Marconi moves to London, England, to find financial support to market his invention in February. He files for the first wireless patent in the world on June 2. William Preece and Marconi conduct the first public demonstration of the wireless at London's Toynbee Hall on December 12.

1897 The Wireless Telegraph and Signal Company is founded.

1899 Marconi transmits a wireless signal across the English Channel on March 27. The Marconi Wireless Telegraph Company of America is founded.

1900 Marconi is granted the "Four Sevens" patent.

1901 Marconi transmits the first transatlantic signal on December 12.

1902 Marconi sends the first lengthy wireless message across the Atlantic Ocean on December 15.

1905 Albert Einstein proposes the theory of relativity.

1905 Marconi marries Beatrice O'Brien on March 16.

1909 U. S. Congress passes the United States Copyright Law.

1909 Marconi is awarded the Nobel Prize in Physics.

1912 The Imperial Wireless Scheme scandal is first reported in July. Marconi loses his right eye following an automobile accident in September.

1912 Marconi operators aboard the *Titanic* use the wireless to send out a distress call on April 15.

1914 World War I begins.

1914 The British government takes control of Marconi's wireless stations in England for the duration of World War I.

1915 Marconi joins the Italian army as a lieutenant after Italy declares war on Germany.

1918 An influenza epidemic spreads across Asia, Europe, and to the Americas, killing 20 million people.

World War I ends.

1922 Marconi predicts the invention of radar during a lecture in New York City on June 20.

1927 Marconi marries Maria Cristina Bezzi-Scali in Rome, Italy, on June 12.

1929 The U.S. stock market crashes on October 29.

1929 Marconi's company and Associated Cable merge to form Cable & Wireless.

1930 Pluto is discovered by astronomers.

1932 Physicists Sir John Douglas Cockcroft and Ernest Walton split the atom for the first time.

1934 Marconi demonstrates blind navigation aboard the *Elettra.*

1935 Marconi is prohibited from defending Italy's Fascist government on British radio.

1937 Marconi dies in Rome, Italy, on July 20.

To Find Out More

BOOKS

Birch, Beverley. *Guglielmo Marconi: Radio Pioneer*. Woodbridge, CT: Blackbirch Press, 2001.

Birch, Beverley. *Marconi's Battle for Radio*. Hauppauge, NY: Barrons Juveniles, 1996.

McCormick, Anita Louise. *The Invention of the Telegraph and Telephone in American History*. Berkeley Heights, NJ: Enslow Publishers, 2004.

Sherrow, Victoria. *Guglielmo Marconi: Inventor of Radio and Wireless Communication*. Berkeley Heights, NJ: Enslow Publishers, 2004.

Weightman, Gavin. *Signor Marconi's Magic Box*. Cambridge, MA: Da Capo Press, 2003.

ORGANIZATIONS AND ONLINE SITES

Guglielmo Marconi Foundation
http://www.fgm.it/ind_f_e.htm

This is the web site of the Guglielmo Marconi Foundation and Museum. The museum is located in Marconi's former home, Villa Griffone.

Hammond Museum of Radio
595 Southgate Road
Guelph, Ontario N1G-3W6
Canada
http://www.kwarc.org/hammond

On this site there is a section dedicated to Marconi and his inventions.

Tuning the World
http://www.tuningtheworld.com

Created by the Canadian Broadcasting Corporation, this site offers a Marconi game for visitors to download and play.

U.S. Marconi Museum
18 North Amherst Road
Bedford, NH 03110
http://www.marconiusa.org/museum

This is the official Web site for the U.S. Marconi Museum, which provides information on Marconi and the history of radio.

A Note on Sources

Written by Italian journalist Giancarlo Masini, *Marconi* (Marsilio Publishers, 1995) is the best available biography dealing with both the life and work of Guglielmo Marconi. More intimate views are offered in *My Father, Marconi* (Guernica Editions, 2002) by his eldest daughter, Degna, and *Marconi My Beloved* (Dante University of America Press, 1999) by his second wife, Maria Cristina. Also strongly recommended is Gavin Weightman's *Signor Marconi's Magic Box* (Da Capo Press, 2003). This lively narrative reads like a biography of the wireless itself, discussing not only Marconi's role in its development, but also the contributions of rival inventors in the United States and Europe. Another wonderful source about Marconi and his inventions is "Marconi Calling" (www.marconicalling.com), a web site assembled by the Marconi Corporation in 1999. The site combines flashy graphics with a wealth of information and photographs documenting the history of wireless technology.

—*Liz Sonneborn*

INDEX

ABOUT THE AUTHOR

Liz Sonneborn is a writer living in Brooklyn, New York. A graduate of Swarthmore College, she has written more than fifty books for children and adults, including *The American West, A to Z of American Women in the Performing Arts,* and *The New York Public Library's Amazing Native American History,* winner of a 2000 Parent's Choice Award.